Teach Me Numbers 1-20

Parents and children of the world, I hope you're ready for a new super star. I created Super Star Teddy. He's the coolest teddy bear ever and a benefit to all children. Super Star Teddy will help children in various areas. He's designed to keep children focus and make learning fun.

This is my third children's book and many more will follow in this collection. I ask all parents to read and review Super Star Teddy. This type of book is needed and as earlier stated, beneficial to children.

Most children start learning their numbers from 1 to 10. Super Star Teddy wants to take children to the next level, because the more a child knows, the better the future will be for her or him. Super Star Teddy is part of my lesson to learn books. Children please make sure you learn your numbers with Super Star Teddy. Thanks so much. Please enjoy reading Super Star Teddy.

By author Anthony Taylor Sr.

Super Star Teddy

Teach Me Numbers 1-20

Hello everyone, I'm Super Star Teddy. I hope you are ready to learn your numbers.

Super Star Teddy will teach and make counting from 1 to 20 very easy. Well, it's time to get started. Super Star Teddy will be in the classroom today. I have many friends. Let's meet my friends and start the lesson for today.

Teach Me Numbers 1-20

Good morning Bobby, I have a question for you. What did your mother put in your lunch today?

Well, Super Star Teddy, I have 1 sandwich, 1 bag of chips, 1 apple and 1 bottle of water.

Bobby you have a great lunch and you are making Super Star Teddy hungry.

1

Teach Me Numbers 1-20

Hey Super Star Teddy, how are you today?

I'm fine Sara. I didn't notice your father's car today.

My parents have 2 cars Super Star Teddy.

Wow, that must be nice! Sara that's wonderful. I wish my parents would have 2 cars.

Super Star Teddy I think you are forgetting that you're a teddy bear.

2

Teach Me Numbers 1-20

Hello Mrs. Jones, you are looking great today.

Thanks Super Star Teddy. You're looking great today as well.

Mrs. Jones what's going on down the hall?

Super Star Teddy have you forgotten about the big book event today?

Yes, you're so right. I did forget. Every book is only 3 dollars.

3

Teach Me Numbers 1-20

Jessica, how are you doing today?

I'm fine Super Star Teddy. How are you doing?

Great and thanks for asking.

Super Star Teddy my birthday is in 4 days.

Jessica are you having a party?

Yes, Super Star Teddy and you're invited.

Thanks for the invite. I'll see you there.

4

Teach Me Numbers 1-20

Super Star Teddy it's so good to see you.

Peter, it's good seeing you again. What have you been up to Peter?

Super Star Teddy I've been doing the same things as before. Just going to school and studying hard. Super Star Teddy I will need your help for my big test in 5 days.

No problem Peter, I'll stop by your house later.

5

Super Star Teddy

Super Star Teddy I have a big problem.

Mr. Mike what's the problem?

I'm missing some frogs for my class project that's coming up on Friday.

Mr. Mike, how many frogs do you still have?

I only have 6 at this time Super Star Teddy.

Well, Mr. Mike your problem is simple. Just use the 6 you have for the class project.

6

Teach Me Numbers 1-20

Super Star Teddy what's your good advice for the day?

Well, Sally my good advice for the day is learning to share.

Wow, Super Star Teddy I was just thinking about that the other day. I know how to share because I have 7 brothers and sisters. I come from a very sharing and caring family.

7

Super Star Teddy

Teach Me Numbers 1-20

Super Star Teddy, Mrs. Gomez is not coming to school today. We don't have a teacher. Will you teach our class Super Star Teddy?

Yes, Roy the school asked me about an hour ago.

Great, I'll run to tell the other students the good news.

Hey, everyone please sit down. I'm Super Star Teddy. I will be your teacher for the day. Here's what I want you to do. Please write 8 ways to be happy and stay happy.

8

Super Star Teddy

Teach Me Numbers 1-20

Super Star Teddy I have a question for you.

Go ahead with your question Tommy.

Does a cat really have 9 lives?

Well, Tommy many people think so, but I must tell you the truth. My answer is no. Tommy do not feel bad about the answer you got. I was told the same thing many years ago.

9

Super Star Teddy

Teach Me Numbers 1-20

Super Star Teddy are we doing great with learning our numbers?

Yes, everyone is doing so well. We have reached number 10 already. Can someone tell me 10 things that come to your mind?

Yes, that is very easy to do Super Star Teddy. Here I go! Dog, Cat, Bird, Car, Truck, House, Donkey, Man, Lady and Super Star Teddy.

10

Super Star Teddy

Teach Me Numbers 1-20

Well, everyone we're at the halfway point. Let us count together and move on.

1 – 2 – 3 – 4 – 5 – 6 – 7 – 8 – 9 – 10

Super Star Teddy

Teach Me Numbers 1-20

Super Star Teddy has to admit that this class of students is very smart. I will pick the student that's number 11 on the class roll for my next question. Lisa this question is all yours. Name a state that starts with the letter T.

Texas starts with the letter T Super Star Teddy.

11

Super Star Teddy

Teach Me Numbers 1-20

We're going to have a fun time today. Why are you so happy James?

Super Star Teddy the class will get our first shipment of computers in today.

How many computers will the class get today James?

We will get 12 today and the others with our next shipment.

12

Teach Me Numbers 1-20

Super Star Teddy will you be attending our field trip in 13 days?

I will try to attend it if I find a replacement for my public speaking event that's on the same day.

13

Super Star Teddy

Teach Me Numbers 1-20

Super Star Teddy have you heard the good news?

What good news Jackie?

This year our school placed first in football out of 14 schools.

Well, Jackie the team's players really worked very hard. They earned their spot.

14

Super Star Teddy my parents have been married for 15 years today. My big brother is 15 years old today and Mrs. Jones has been teaching at this school for 15 years as of today.

That's a lot of good things that happened 15 years ago Tina.

15

Teach Me Numbers 1-20

Terry what's in your bag?

I have a bag of 16 apples and they were on sale.

How much were they Terry?

I only spent a dollar for 16 apples. I think it's a great deal. Super Star Teddy what do you think?

Yes, that's a wonderful deal.

Super Star Teddy would you like an apple?

Yes, I do Terry. Thanks so much.

16

Teach Me Numbers 1-20

How are you doing today Super Star Teddy?

I'm fine Mrs. Jones. How's your day going so far?

My day has been busy, but it's Thursday and the week is almost over.

Mrs. Jones this year is moving very fast and will be over in 17 days.

I know Super Star Teddy. What plans do you have for the summer?

Mrs. Jones I'll do what most teddy bears do. I will find me a corner of a room to hang out.

17

Teach Me Numbers 1-20

We voted last week for a class president and the whole class is shocked about the outcome. The majority of the students voted for the new class president. The new class president received 18 students' votes. Most of the students say voting can be hard if you select the wrong person. Here at our school, they teach us what voting really means. We will be trained to select the right person for the job when we reach grade school.

18

Super Star Teddy are you going to the big party that's happening in 19 days at Sugar Land park?

Yes, I'll be there. I never miss that big event. I always have a great time. Paul have you and your family ever been to the big event?

No, Super Star Teddy my family and I have only been in Texas a few months.

19

Super Star Teddy

Teach Me Numbers 1-20

Mrs. Jones I would like to thank you and your 20 students. You all have helped Super Star Teddy complete my first of the Super Star Teddy collection. I'm so proud of your class. I really look forward to working with you and your future classes as well. Teach me numbers should help children all over the world. Counting from 1 to 20 will help many children think beyond the normal at an early age.

20

Super Star Teddy

Well, everyone we have made it to the end of Teach Me Numbers. Now it's time to shout the numbers out!

1 – 2 – 3 – 4 – 5 – 6 – 7 – 8 – 9 – 10 – 11 – 12 – 13 – 14 – 15 – 16 – 17 – 18 – 19 – 20!

Thanks to everyone and please check out Super Star Teddy's next book that's coming out soon.

Contact author Anthony Taylor Sr. at:

PO Box 31054
Houston, TX 77231

Email: anthonybestbooks@protonmail.com

Super Star Notes

Super Star Notes

Super Star Notes

Super Star Notes

Super Star Notes

Super Star Notes